T0026666

LIKE NO OTHER

EARTH'S COOLEST ONE-OF-A-KIND CREATURES

Sneed B. Collard III
Illustrated by Christopher Silas Neal

KANE PRESS
AN IMPRINT OF ASTRA BOOKS FOR YOUNG READERS
New York

Order Carnivora (Carnivore)

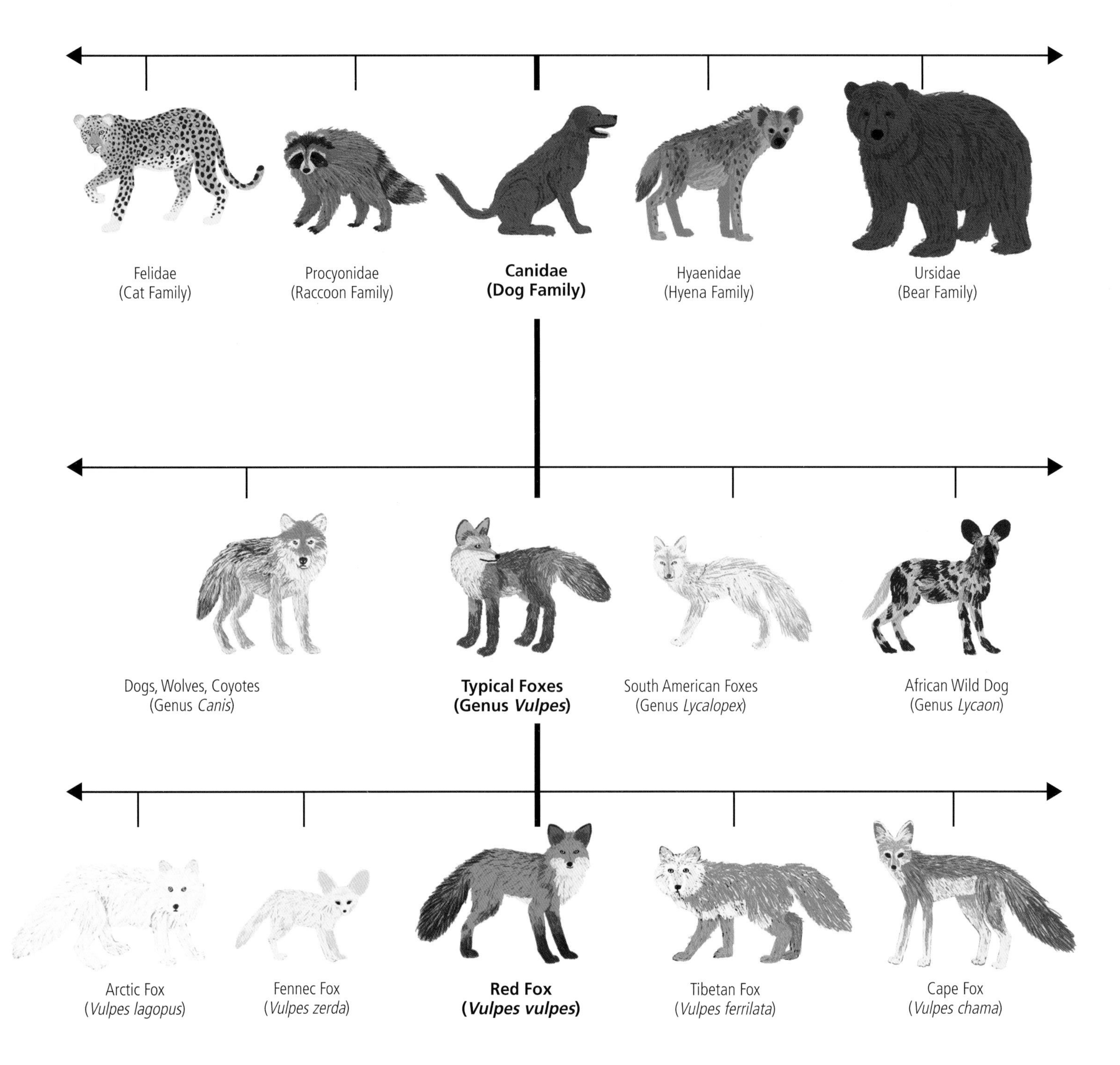

The One-of-a-Kind Club

On a cool New Zealand evening, a handsome gray reptile pokes its head from an underground burrow. It is a *tuatara* (TWO-uh-TAR-uh), the last survivor of a once huge group of reptiles. That makes the tuatara an animal like no other. A one-of-a-kind creature.

One of a kind, but not alone.

Scientists group—or classify—living things by how closely related they are. Most kinds of animals have both close and more distant relatives. Take the red fox. The red fox is closely related to several other kinds, or *species*, of foxes. Scientists put them together in the same tight group, or *genus*, called *Vulpes* (a Latin word meaning "foxes"). Foxes are also related to dogs and wolves, though not quite as much, so they all get grouped in the same scientific *family*, the dog family. The dog family, in turn, belongs to a larger scientific *order*, the Carnivora, which it shares with cats, bears, and other animal groups. And yet the Carnivora are only one of many orders of mammals!

Unlike the red fox, however, the animals in this book have no close living relatives. Some may never have had close relatives. For others—such as the tuatara, secretarybird, and platypus—their last close relatives became extinct. This makes the creatures in this book truly different and some of the most interesting animals on the planet.

Secretarybird

Getting a Kick Out of Life

Africa's secretarybird may be Earth's most unusual raptor, or bird of prey. Why? It pursues its food not by flying, but on foot. Even more astonishing, it usually kicks and stomps larger prey to death! Insects, frogs, mongooses, chickens—even poisonous snakes—fall victim to its deadly, flashing feet.

- Long ago the ancestors of secretarybirds split off from hawks, eagles, and other birds of prey. Scientists have found ancient fossils of secretarybird relatives, but none of them live today. The bird sits alone in its own scientific family, the Sagittariidae (SAJ-ih-TARE-ih-dee).
- Secretarybirds live in short, open grasslands and savannas in many parts of Africa. They often nest in the tops of flat-topped acacia trees.
- Farmers value secretarybirds because they hunt snakes, rodents, and other pests. They swallow most prey whole.
- Even though they hunt mostly on foot, secretarybirds can fly, and sometimes kill snakes by dropping them from the air.
- The name secretarybird probably comes from the resemblance of its crest to a bunch of quill pens stuck behind the ear.

Height: about 4 feet
Weight: 5 to 9.5 pounds
Lifespan: 10 to 15 years in the wild

Platypus

Venomous Egg-Layer

A bill like a duck. Spurs that inject painful venom. And it *lays eggs*! Meet Australia's platypus—Earth's ultimate one-of-a-kind creature.

- The platypus belongs to the *monotremes* (MO-no-treemz), which split off from all other mammals about one hundred and sixty-six million years ago. This was during the Jurassic Period, when dinosaurs dominated the Earth. Monotremes thrived for millions of years, but only five species remain today: four spiny echidnas and the only member of the family Ornithorhynchidae (or-ni-thoe-RINKE-ih-dee)—the platypus.

- Other mammals give birth to live young, but monotremes lay eggs. A platypus digs a nesting burrow in an Australian stream bank and packs it with soft plant material. Then she lays one to three marble-sized eggs.
- After hatching, the platypups nurse on mother's milk for about four months before heading out to hunt on their own.
- Platypuses use their sensitive bills to locate prey in shallow waters. They detect movement and electric currents made by insect larvae, crayfish, worms, and other animals.
- A venomous spur about half an inch long sticks out from each rear ankle of a male platypus—a formidable weapon for fights with other males over mates or territories.

Length: about 1.5 feet
Weight: 1.5 to 6.5 pounds
Lifespan: 6 to 15 years in the wild

Aye-Aye

Finger Food

A character from *Star Wars*? Nope, but the strange-looking aye-aye (pronounced "I-I") may be the world's most unusual primate.

- Aye-ayes are lemurs that live in forests, but also feed in farms and plantations. They are the world's largest nocturnal primates.
- Like other kinds of lemurs, aye-ayes live on the island nation of Madagascar—but aye-ayes are not closely related to other lemurs. They evolved away from them 50 million years ago and now reside alone in their own scientific family, the Daubentoniidae (daw-ben-TONE-ee-ih-dee).

- Aye-ayes eat fruits, and also target insect grubs inside of trees. They find prey by using a tool no other animal has—a very long third finger. With this finger, aye-ayes tap on a tree, and listen to the echo. When they detect an insect or a hollow cavity, they tear into the tree with their impressive incisor teeth and use their long claws to "fish out" their prey.
- Aye-ayes' incisors keep growing all their lives. This is rare in the world of mammals, and led early scientists to believe that aye-ayes were rodents, not primates.
- Aye-ayes are harmless to people, but superstitions made many people fear aye-ayes and sometimes kill them. Others value aye-ayes for eating forest and farm pests.

Length: about 15 inches, with a bushy tail longer than its body
Weight: 5.5 to 6.2 pounds
Lifespan: about 20 years in the wild

Whale Shark

Gentle Giant

The whale shark is the world's largest fish. It outgrows its closest competitor, the basking shark, by fifteen feet. It would take about a dozen large great white sharks to equal the weight of the largest whale shark.

- Despite its size, the whale shark eats some of the ocean's smallest prey, including tiny shrimplike animals, eggs of corals, fish eggs, small fish, and more. Some other sharks also do this, but scientists place the whale shark in its own family, the Rhincodontidae (RHINE-co-DAWN-tih-dee).
- A whale shark collects food by swimming near the surface with its mouth open—or engulfs schools of tiny fish and other critters in quick gulps. It uses special filters near its gills to trap and gather food.
- Whale sharks produce eggs that hatch inside the mother's body. Scientists found 304 shark embryos inside of one pregnant female—a record for a shark.
- Whale sharks live in the warmer oceans of the world. They usually swim alone, but tourists and divers flock to some coastal locations where more than a hundred sharks may gather to feed.

Length: can grow longer than 60 feet; most 13 to 16 feet
Weight: up to 79,000 pounds, most less than half
Lifespan: unknown, but estimated at 70 to 100 years

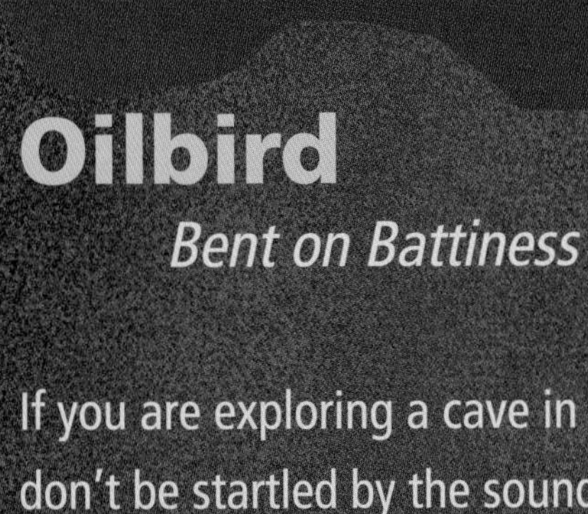

Oilbird

Bent on Battiness

If you are exploring a cave in the western mountains of South America, don't be startled by the sound of flapping wings. Bats? Perhaps. But you also could have just heard another unique—or one-of-a-kind—bird: the oilbird.

- The oilbird is the only living species in the bird family Steatornithidae (stee-ah-tore-NITH-ih-dee). Fifty million-year-old fossils of oilbird ancestors have been found in Wyoming—evidence that this family also once lived in North America.
- Oilbird pairs build platform nests inside caves. One cave in Venezuela holds between ten and eighteen *thousand* oilbirds!
- Oilbirds eat only fruit. The birds locate food by sight and smell in the forest at night.

- Oilbirds have some of the most sensitive eyes of any animal. Like bats, they also use *echolocation* to find their way in the dark. They make sounds and listen to where the echoes come from to detect objects around them.
- The high fat, or oil, content in their bodies gives oilbirds their name. They contain so much oil that people once boiled down the extra-plump chicks to make fuel for oil lamps.

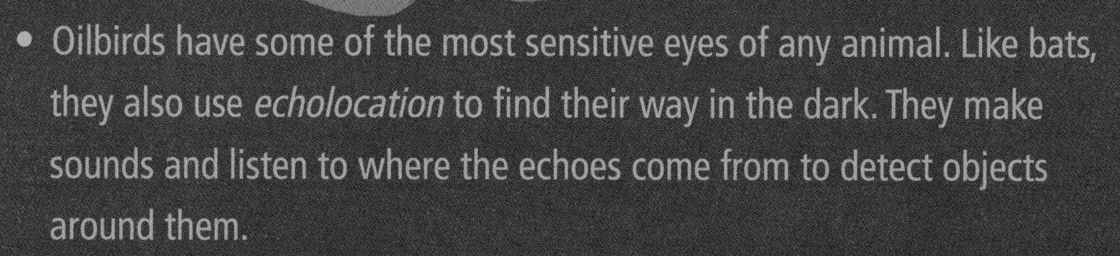

Length: 16 to 19 inches
Weight: about a pound
Lifespan: unknown

Purple Frog

Earthworm Amphibian

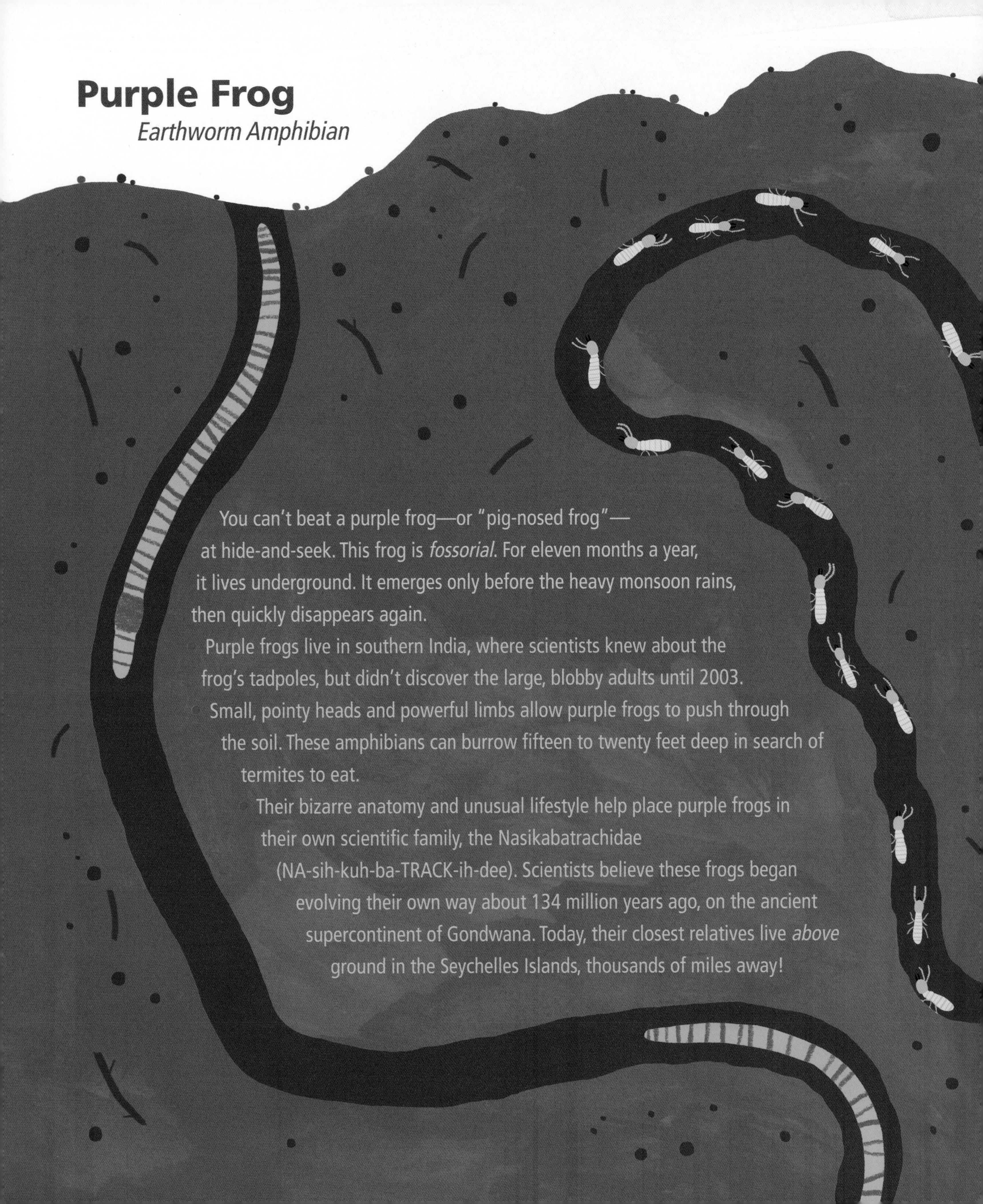

You can't beat a purple frog—or "pig-nosed frog"—at hide-and-seek. This frog is *fossorial*. For eleven months a year, it lives underground. It emerges only before the heavy monsoon rains, then quickly disappears again.

Purple frogs live in southern India, where scientists knew about the frog's tadpoles, but didn't discover the large, blobby adults until 2003.

Small, pointy heads and powerful limbs allow purple frogs to push through the soil. These amphibians can burrow fifteen to twenty feet deep in search of termites to eat.

Their bizarre anatomy and unusual lifestyle help place purple frogs in their own scientific family, the Nasikabatrachidae (NA-sih-kuh-ba-TRACK-ih-dee). Scientists believe these frogs began evolving their own way about 134 million years ago, on the ancient supercontinent of Gondwana. Today, their closest relatives live *above* ground in the Seychelles Islands, thousands of miles away!

During mating, a male crawls onto a female's back and holds on. In nearby pools, the female releases up to three thousand eggs as the male fertilizes them. The purple frog's tadpoles live in fast-flowing streams where other tadpoles would get swept away. When they change, or metamorphose, into adults they leave the stream and dig into their new underground lifestyles.

Length: 2 to 3 inches
Weight: about an ounce
Lifespan: unknown, but probably 7 to 10 years

Walrus

Tooth Walker

They are the world's third-largest seal—but it's those ivory tusks that truly set walruses apart. Tusks make walruses look incredibly comical. They come in incredibly handy, too.

- Scientists put the walrus in its own family, the Odobenidae (o-doh-BEN-ih-dee), which split off from other seals about 15 to 20 million years ago. Other, extinct Odobenidae remain only as fossils.
- Walruses live in subarctic and arctic seas. Thick blubber keeps them warm. They feed by diving to shallow sea bottoms for clams and other shellfish. A walrus can dive to more than 1,600 feet, but most dives are much shallower and last five to seven minutes.
- Walruses apparently do not use their tusks for feeding. Instead, they suction up prey with their lips and other mouthparts. One scientific team observed a walrus scooping up an average of fifty-three clams on each dive!

- Walruses *do* use their tusks to help pull themselves up onto ice floes. This is sometimes called "tooth walking." Male walruses also use tusks in brutal fights with rival males.
- A thousand years ago, Vikings in Greenland hunted walrus for their ivory tusks. The US and Canada ban most trade in walrus ivory today.

Length: 9 to 10.5 feet
Weight: 1,900 to 2,700 pounds
Lifespan: 30 to 40 years

Pronghorn

Outracing the Ice Age

Coyotes can't catch it. Mountain lions? Eat my dust! Even people in cars have trouble keeping up with it. It is an animal separate from all others, North America's pronghorn—a mammal that, mysteriously, is faster than it needs to be.

- Pronghorns resemble antelopes living in Africa and Asia, but are in their own family, the Antilocapridae (an-tih-lo-CAP-rih-dee). During recent Ice Ages, other members of this family lived in North America, but today the pronghorn's closest living relatives are Africa's giraffes and okapis.
- Pronghorns live in grass, shrub, and desert areas from southern Canada to northern Mexico. They feed on many different plants, but especially sagebrush.
- Adult pronghorns have been clocked at 60 miles per hour, the fastest speed of any hoofed mammal. They can keep running fast longer than any other animal. Why the speed? Scientists believe pronghorns evolved during a time of superfast predators, such as large American cheetah-like cats. Those predators have gone extinct, but the pronghorn hasn't slowed down.

Height: 2.5 to 3.5 feet at shoulder
Weight: 75 to 150 pounds
Lifespan: about 5 to 9 years in the wild

Leatherback Sea Turtle

Deep-Dinner Diving

The leatherback not only looks different from all other sea turtles. It *is* different. It has a rubbery, flexible shell. It can dive almost a mile deep. Most obvious, it is more than twice as big as the next biggest sea turtle.

- Leatherbacks are Earth's largest turtles. Most sea turtles grow to two or three feet long and weigh 100 to 300 pounds. Leatherbacks can grow more than six feet long and can weigh more than *half a ton*.
- The turtle gets its name from its tough, flexible covering. This shell can bend and change shape. That may prevent it from cracking or breaking under the extreme pressures of ocean depths. Leatherbacks swim in their own turtle family, Dermochelyidae (derm-oh-KEE-lee-uh-dee).
- Leatherbacks eat jellyfish and similar creatures. The turtles usually feed within 330 feet of the surface, but scientists have recorded dives of almost 4,000 feet deep.
- These turtles live in all of the world's oceans, and regularly travel thousands of miles between nesting beaches and feeding grounds. Some leatherbacks that breed in Asia feed off the coast of California.
- Unlike most other turtles, leatherbacks are warm-blooded, allowing them to explore cooler places such as Canada and Alaska.

Length: up to 6 or 7 feet
Weight: up to 1,300 pounds
Lifespan: unknown, perhaps 50 years and older

Monito del Monte

Adorable Ancient Marsupial

In southern Argentina and Chile lives an adorable mouselike mammal called the monito del monte, or "little monkey of the mountain." But this animal is neither monkey nor mouse. It is the sole survivor of an ancient group of marsupials.

- Marsupial mammals probably arose in South America 60 or 70 million years ago when it was joined to Antarctica and Australia as the ancient supercontinent of Gondwana. Some marsupials, such as kangaroo ancestors, reached Australia. The monito del monte is the last member of a group that mostly stayed behind—the scientific order Microbiotheria (mi-cro-bi-oh-THEAR-ee-uh), a name that means "small living beast."
- Like other marsupials, the monito del monte gives birth to babies that are not fully developed. These crawl into a pouch and grow by feeding on mother's milk.
- The monito del monte lives in cool, or temperate, bamboo and other forests. When temperatures dip it goes into torpor, a kind of hibernation that can last a few hours or many days.
- The monito del monte eats insects and fruit. It probably plays a key role in spreading the seeds of many forest plants—including seeds too large for birds to swallow and spread.

Length: about 7 to 10 inches
Weight: about an ounce
Lifespan: probably 3 to 4 years

Kakapo

Walking Through Time

New Zealand's kakapo is the world's largest parrot. That is fascinating by itself—but what is even more interesting is that *the kakapo can't fly*!

- Kakapos are one of several New Zealand birds that evolved to become flightless. They include the famous kiwi birds and a group of large, extinct birds called moas. Kakapos may have evolved to be flightless because, before humans arrived, New Zealand had no major mammalian predators. Flight may have offered few advantages to some birds and, over time, they lost their abilities to fly.
- Kakapos are nocturnal and use their good sense of smell to find things in the dark. They give off a sweet odor, perhaps so other kakapos can locate them.
- Kakapo beaks are especially adapted for grinding up leaves, seeds, roots, fruits, and other plant material. The birds get enough energy to breed and raise babies only when native trees produce an especially large number of fruits and seeds.
- Two other New Zealand birds, the kea and kaka, are part of the same bird family as the kakapo—the Strigopidae (strih-JOP-ih-dee). Both of these parrots can fly, but scientists believe they split from the kakapo's ancestors 28 to 29 million years ago.
- Scientists have found fossils of an even larger flightless New Zealand parrot. This extinct parrot weighed about fifteen pounds and stood almost as tall as a person's waist!

Height: about two feet
Weight: 3 to 5 pounds
Lifespan: unknown, probably
50 to 100+ years

Tuatara

Fleeing Pangea

Still wondering about the critter we met on the first page? The tuatara belongs to an order of reptiles called Rhynchocephalians (RHYNK-oh-seh-FAIL-ee-enz). 200 million years ago, many kinds of Rhynchocephalians lived on Earth, but today the tuatara is the very last of their kind.

- Rhynchocephalians evolved when most of the continents—including Gondwana—were part of a giant supercontinent called Pangea (pan-JEE-uh). Over time, many Rhynchocephalians became extinct. Mammals and other animals may have eaten or outcompeted them. Before this could happen to the tuatara's ancestors, however, the islands of New Zealand drifted away from Gondwana, carrying the reptiles to safety.
- Rhynchocephalia means "beakhead." The name comes from a beak-like tip on the animals' upper jaws.
- Tuatara often live with nesting seabirds, moving into their burrows and eating their eggs and chicks. Tuatara also eat large cricket-like insects called wetas.
- Rare for a reptile, the tuatara's body keeps working at temperatures as low as 43ºF—an adaptation to New Zealand's chilly climate.
- Humans brought deadly rats, cats, and other predators to New Zealand. These invasive species wiped out tuatara from the country's main islands, but the reptiles have survived on smaller islands with fewer predators.

Length: up to 2 feet

Weight: about 2.2 pounds

Lifespan: 50 to 100+ years

Humans

Reshaping the Planet

Many more amazing one-of-a-kind animals live on Earth. One-of-a-kind plants, too. But we can't leave out a last example—humans.

- During the past several million years, several different kinds of humans have lived on Earth. These include *Homo floresiensis*—nicknamed "hobbits"—a kind of human that stood less than four feet tall and lived only about 100,000 to 50,000 years ago. Scientists know about *Homo floresiensis* and other humans from bones, tools, and other clues that various human species left behind.
- The first humans walked the Earth about 2 to 2.5 million years ago. As recently as 40,000 years ago, other human species lived along with us. We don't know why the others disappeared, but today our own species—*Homo sapiens*—are the last humans on the planet. Our closest living relatives? Chimpanzees, gorillas, and orangutans—which, with us, belong to the scientific family Hominidae (haw-MIN-ih-dee).

- Humans' big brains and useful hands have allowed people to invent countless useful tools, clothing, and other objects. Our ability to speak has helped us live in societies where we can work together to survive.
- Human intelligence and skills have also gotten us into trouble. As we continue to invent things and increase our population, we have damaged and overheated the planet—the problem known as *climate change*. Frequent wars have caused huge harm to ourselves and our environment.
- By learning from our mistakes—and doing things differently—we can change. We need to keep educating ourselves, talk to each other, and understand that *all* species share Planet Earth together.

Average Adult Height: about 5 feet 7 inches
Average Adult Weight: about 136 pounds
Average Lifespan: about 73 years

Saving One-of-a-Kind Creatures

The ancestors of most one-of-a-kind animals have survived for millions of years, through ice ages, continental collisions, volcanic activity, and more. However, in just the past two hundred years our human population has grown from about one billion to eight billion. To feed, clothe, and house all of us, people gobble up a huge chunk of Earth's land, water, forests, and other resources. This leaves very little room and resources for wildlife. But our impacts don't stop there. Humans have helped spread cats, rats, carp, and thousands of other invasive species that outcompete and kill native animals and plants. Human factories and vehicles pollute air, oceans, and rivers. They also release carbon dioxide that is drastically increasing Earth's temperatures through climate change. This is actually destroying and shifting habitats where wild animals and plants live.

The good news? Humans can—and are—fighting back!

In New Zealand, for instance, efforts to control invasive rats, cats, and other species have helped the kakapo come back from the brink of extinction. Tuatara populations are also rebounding.

The number one best thing we can do for animals is to reduce our "carbon footprint"—the amount of energy we use. Simply turning out a light reduces how much coal, gas, and other fossil fuels we burn to create electricity. Saying no to a plastic bag at a store saves the energy and materials needed to make another bag to replace it. Urging politicians to force large, polluting companies to be more environmentally responsible makes an even greater impact.

There are dozens of other things we all can do to help Earth's one-of-a-kind creatures. To get some ideas, try searching for "climate change," "preventing pollution," "protecting biodiversity," or "stopping invasive species" on reputable sites such as those of the Environmental Protection Agency, NOAA (National Oceanic and Atmospheric Administration), and National Geographic Kids.

Efforts to protect animals and our environment have already made a huge difference in the world. Your efforts will, too.

Be an Animal Scientist

Since humans began, we have studied the natural world and tried to figure out relationships around us. In the 4th century BCE, the Greek philosopher Aristotle came up with a classification system for animals and plants. In the mid-1700s, Swedish botanist Carl Linnaeus developed our modern system of classifying and naming living things. Today, scientists called taxonomists still work hard to identify and group what we see around us. You can too! Study this forest scene and see if you can group animals and plants by how closely related they look.

- **Step One**: Examine the living things in the illustrations. Take out a notebook and write down some categories to place each living thing in. To help you choose categories, ask yourself questions such as:
    1. Is this an animal, plant, or something else?
    2. Does it have legs? How many?
    3. Does it fly?
    4. Is this tall or short?
    5. What kind of leaves does this have?
    6. Does it have hair, fur, feathers, or scales?

- **Step Two**: Place each living thing into one of your categories.

- **Step Three**: As your powers of observation get better and more detailed, modify or add to your categories. You may want to divide one category up into two others—or lump two categories together. You might even replace a category with a more useful one.

- **Step Four**: Compare your categories with what a friend or family member came up with. Did you agree on some categories? Did one category have more kinds of living things than another? Why do you think it is?

Figuring Out Relatives

Taxonomy is the science of grouping and naming living things based on how related they are. Scientists don't always agree on how closely related two animals might be. However, powerful new tools now can examine our DNA—the instructions inside our cells that shape how we grow and function. Living things that share more of the same DNA usually are more closely related than other species. That is helping scientists unravel relationships between species.

To understand more about how scientists group living things, look at the table below. The left column lists the different taxonomic groups (from the largest group to smallest) that scientists use to organize—or classify—living things. Kingdoms are the biggest groups, containing the most kinds of living things, and each group gets smaller as you go down from there. The four other columns list animals from this book and which taxonomic groups scientists place each one into.

	Human	**Aye-aye**	**Platypus**	**Whale Shark**
Kingdom	Animalia	Animalia	Animalia	Animalia
Phylum	Chordata	Chordata	Chordata	Chordata
Class	Mammalia	Mammalia	Mammalia	Chondricthyes
Order	Primates	Primates	Monotremata	Orectolobiformes
Family	Hominidae	Daubentoniidae	Ornithorhynchidae	Rhincodontidae
Genus	*Homo*	*Daubentonia*	*Ornithorhynchus*	*Rhincodon*
Species	*sapiens*	*madagascariensis*	*anatinus*	*typus*

Some Questions to Answer

- If you look at the table, do you see any groups that all four animals belong to? Can you guess what any of the group names mean, such as Animalia or Mammalia? (Hint: If an animal is in "Chordata" it means that the animal has a spinal cord.)

- Are there any groups, such as Mammalia or Primates, that include some of the four animals—but not others? What do you think that means? Are some of the four animals more closely related than others?

- An animal's scientific name consists of only the last two groups it belongs to, its *genus* (JEE-nus) and *species*. Do you notice two unusual things about how a scientific name is written, a name such as *Ornithorhynchus anatinus*?

- Chondrichthyes is the class of animals that includes sharks and rays. How many of the animals in the chart belong in this class? Can you think of some other animals that might go into this group?

- Which order do scientists place humans and aye-ayes in? Do any of the other animals in the table belong to that same order? Do you think that means they are more closely or more distantly related to humans and aye-ayes?

One-of-a-Kind Words to Know

Class: In science, a larger group of species (larger than order and family) that are somewhat—but not too closely—related.

Family: In science, a medium-size group of species that are somewhat—but not too closely—related.

Gondwana: An ancient supercontinent that consisted of Africa, Antarctica, South America, India, Australia, and New Zealand. It completed its break up 60–80 million years ago.

Kingdom: A scientific grouping that includes a *very* large number and variety of living things that have a few basic features in common.

Order: In science, a group of species that is larger than a family, but still all have some common features.

Pangea: An ancient supercontinent consisting of the land masses of Gondwana plus North America and Asia.

Phylum: A very large grouping of animals, such as all animals that have backbones.

Researching *Like No Other*—for Teachers and Parents

To research this book, I relied mainly on articles published in scientific journals, as well as books, popular magazine and newspaper articles, and reputable websites. I also contacted scientists directly with questions. You can find my complete reference list on my website, sneedbcollardiii.com.

It's worth noting that scientists don't always agree about how closely one animal is related to other animals. In these cases, I looked for what I considered the most reliable information or what most scientists seemed to agree on. The purple frog provides a good example. Some scientists believe there are two species of purple frog living in different regions. Other scientists are not convinced they are separate species. After reading the arguments and talking to a purple frog expert in India, neither was I, and I chose to keep the frog in the book—but that may change in the future. As scientists continue to make new discoveries, our understanding of relationships between species will keep changing.

Learning More About One-of-a-Kind Animals—for Kids

Some of the animals in this book are well-known, including walruses, pronghorns, platypuses, whale sharks, and leatherback sea turtles. A simple library or web search will reveal numerous children's and adult books and articles that can give you more information.

Watch out for out-of-date or exaggerated information. Take the leatherback sea turtle. You might find the maximum length for this animal listed as nine or ten feet, but very few of the turtles ever reach this size. A typical maximum length is more like six to seven feet. Compare sources before deciding how big an animal is or how long it might live.

Many websites also contain incorrect information, but some websites from government agencies and other groups are especially reliable. Examples of websites you can trust are:

- U. S. Fish & Wildlife Service: fws.gov/species/search

- The International Union for Conservation of Nature (IUCN) Red List of Threatened Species: iucnredlist.org/en

- Cornell Lab of Ornithology's *Birds of the World:* birdsoftheworld.org/bow/home (Subscription required—your public or nearby university library may have one.)

- Smithsonian Natural History Museum: naturalhistory.si.edu/

- National Oceanic and Atmospheric Administration: fisheries.noaa.gov/find-species

- New Zealand Department of Conservation: doc.govt.nz/

The above websites are especially useful to learn more about some of the lesser-known animals in this book, such as the kakapo, tuatara, and monito del monte.

You can also look up scientific articles about animals yourself. These may not be available at your school library, but should be available at your public library and any college libraries near you. Ask the reference librarian there how to do this. Some scientific articles are difficult to understand, but if you love animals like I do, you still will be able to learn a lot from them.

More One-of-a-Kind Animals

Earth has many other animals with no close relatives—animals we could not squeeze into this book. Besides the animals you recognize from this book, can you spot any other one-of-a-kind animals on the map?

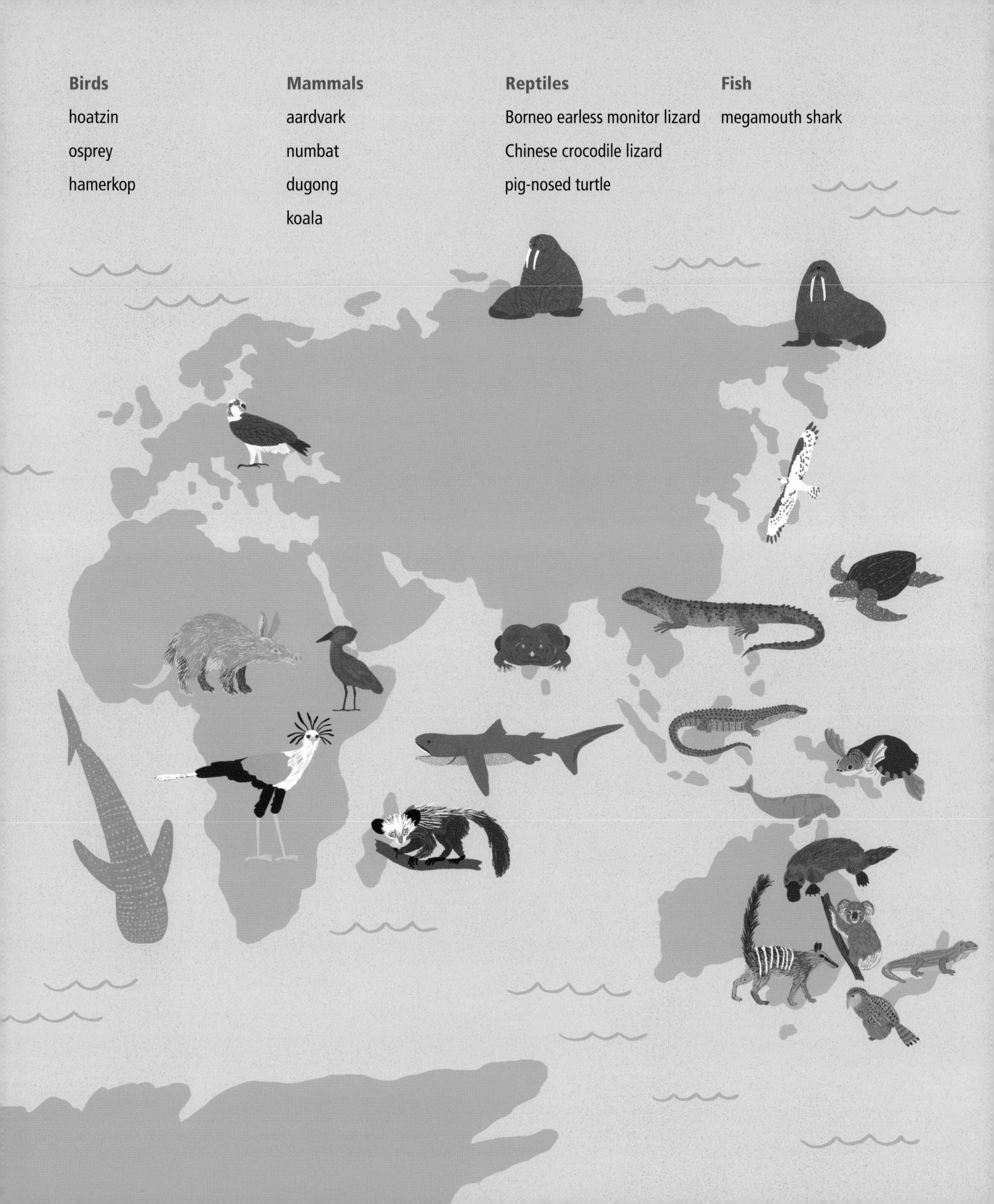
Birds
hoatzin
osprey
hamerkop
Mammals
aardvark
numbat
dugong
koala
Reptiles
Borneo earless monitor lizard
Chinese crocodile lizard
pig-nosed turtle
Fish
megamouth shark

Thank you!

Learning and writing about one-of-a-kind animals has been a one-of-a-kind experience, and I got a lot of help along the way. I'd like to thank the following scientists who helped me track down hard-to-find information: Ronald Pine (mammals), Mollie Bloomsmith (primates), Dean Gibson (aye-ayes), Ashish Thomas (purple frogs), and Diego F. Cisneros-Heredia (oilbirds). An especially big shout out to Ronald Pine for his expert critique and feedback on the entire book, and to my one-of-a-kind editor, Harold Underdown, for his unflagging enthusiasm and effort on this project.

In memory of my high school biology teacher, Lelin Miller, who taught me about slime molds.

—*SBC III*

For Jasper and River—*CSN*

Kane Press
An imprint of Astra Books for Young Readers, a division of Astra Publishing House
astrapublishinghouse.com
Printed in Malaysia

Library of Congress Cataloging-in-Publication Data

Names: Collard, Sneed B., author. | Neal, Christopher Silas, illustrator.
Title: Like no other : earth's coolest one-of-a-kind creatures / Sneed B. Collard III ; illustrated by Christopher Silas Neal.
Description: First edition. | New York : Kane Press, [2024] | Summary: "A survey of thirteen unusual animals, from the secretarybird to the tuatara, unique due to their adaptations and isolation on their own branch of the evolutionary tree. Includes a map, glossary, and recommended resources"-- Provided by publisher.
Identifiers: LCCN 2023022906 (print) | LCCN 2023022907 (ebook) | ISBN 9781662670077 (hardcover) | ISBN 9781662670084 (ebk)
Subjects: LCSH: Animals--Juvenile literature. | Animals--Adaptation--Juvenile literature.
Classification: LCC QL49 .C6733 2024 (print) | LCC QL49 (ebook) | DDC 590--dc23/eng/20230713
LC record available at https://lccn.loc.gov/2023022906
LC ebook record available at https://lccn.loc.gov/2023022907

First edition
10 9 8 7 6 5 4 3 2 1

Design by Barbara Grzeslo. The text is set in Frutiger LT Std 57 Condensed. The titles are set in Frutiger LT Std 75 Black. The illustrations are mixed media, including acrylic, pencil, and digital.

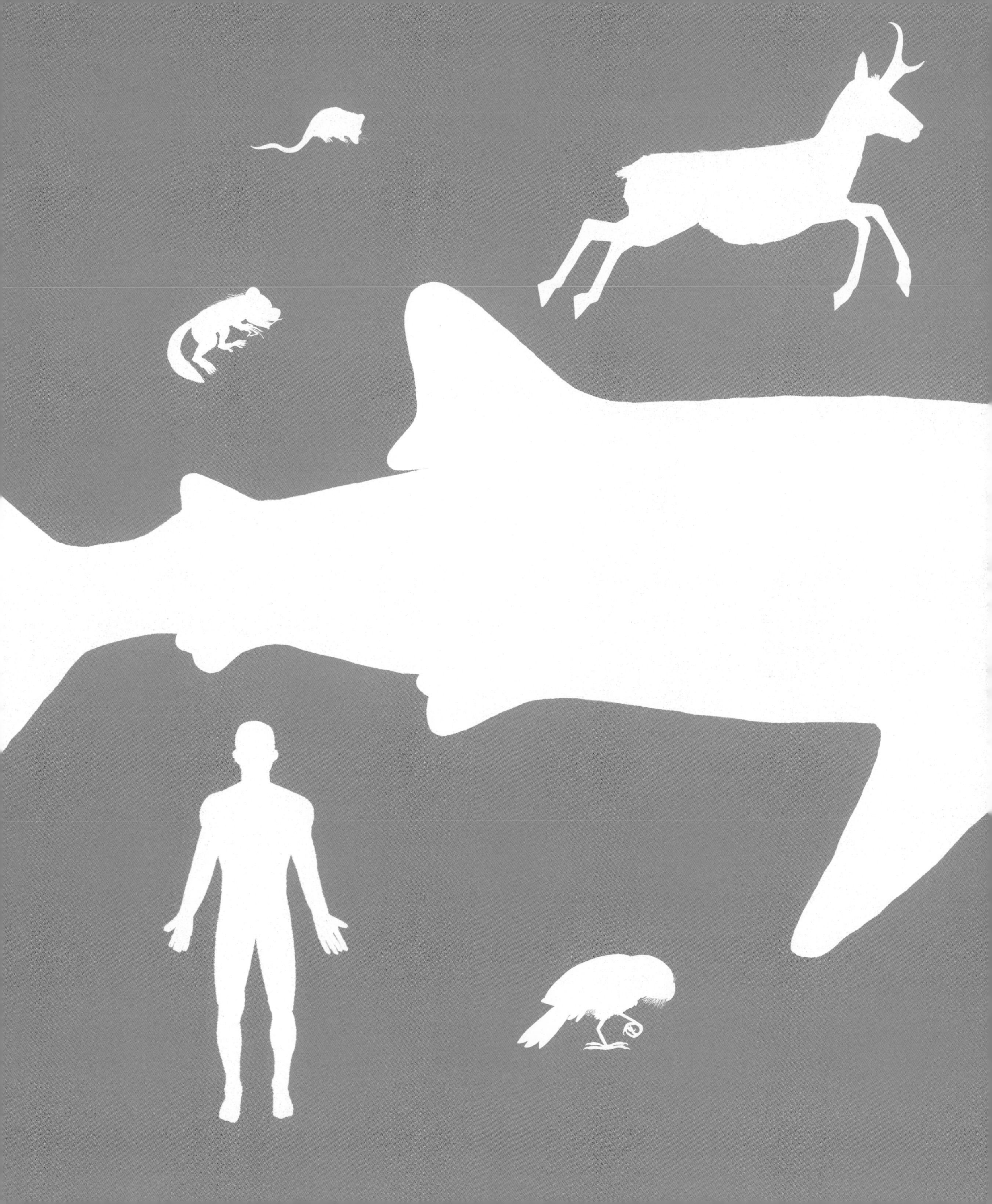